7

DAYS TO SUCCESS IN

SKIING

7
DAYS TO SUCCESS IN

SKIING

**ALEX
LEAF**

CRESCENT BOOKS
New York/Avenel, New Jersey

This 1992 edition published by Crescent Books,
distributed by Outlet Book Company, Inc.,
a Random House Company,
40 Engelhard Avenue,
Avenel, New Jersey 07001.

ISBN 0 517 08643 3

Printed and bound in Belgium

87654321

Credits

MANAGING EDITOR: Anne McDowall
EDITOR: Sean Callery
DESIGNER: Tim Scott
ILLUSTRATOR: Tony Randell
MODELS: Debbie Lambert and Alex Leaf
TYPESET BY: SX Composing Ltd.
COLOUR SEPARATION BY: P & W Graphics
Pte. Ltd.
PRINTED IN BELGIUM BY: Proost International
Book Production, Turnhout.

Acknowledgments

The author and publishers would like to thank
the following for their help in the preparation of
this book:

Badger Sports, London Ltd.; Copper Mountain
Resort, Colorado; Martyn Hurn; Debbie and
Tony Lambert of Ski Fever Holidays; Sheena
Leaf; Ron Batley of Wessex Ski Club, Torquay;
World Class Skiing.

CONTENTS

· ·

INTRODUCTION

Skiing is a great sport for people of all ages and abilities. You can make it as competitive or as leisurely as you wish: for some people, just enjoying the atmosphere of the mountains is enough reason to take it up. Within skiing you will discover many joys that are difficult to find in everyday life – particularly a marvellous sense of freedom, and a sense of discovering new territories. Whatever your aspirations as a skier, you will find enjoyment within yourself. If you are not keen on competing with other skiers then this sport is still ideal for you.

This book aims to make your first efforts on the slopes easier and more successful. The clear photographs, artwork and simple explanations clearly show the areas on which to concentrate. The information is what your first instructor is likely to teach you. Some explanations may change from instructor to instructor, and country to country, but the basics of good ski technique remain the same.

Of course no two people are identical, but in relation to gravity we all are! The techniques and exercises in this book aim to encourage the use of gravity in harmony with the human body. Using only the natural forces and harnessing these with the body will make you an effective skier.

Skiing as free expression

Ski teaching has come a long way from the early days of wooden skis and leather lace-up boots. For many years there was a set pattern of ski techniques which had to be adhered to so that you skied as your instructor skied: parallel and feet together. However, many countries have taken up the sport and adopted a forward-thinking approach to encourage new ideas to assist the learning skier. Today skiing is more of a vehicle for free expression. It is therefore important that your instructor is able to understand you as an individual. Finding the right clothing and equipment also plays an important role. Ensure your clothing is of a good standard and that the equipment is safe.

Basic fitness is very useful to ensure enjoyment on your first ski trip. You should begin a programme to improve flexibility and stamina, including aerobic exercises, before you go. Seek advice from a fitness coach on the programme best suited to your individual needs.

OPPOSITE: *Skiing gives you the freedom of the mountains, and much more. You may feel that all you want to do is get about the mountain safely. However, once you reach that goal, the hunger to improve your ski technique is likely to push you further. Skiing freely and effortlessly takes perseverance, but it is not beyond the reach of anyone who takes up the sport with enthusiasm. Feeling good and confident about yourself is the doorway to achieving your aims. The benefits go beyond the sport: you can improve your outlook on life and gain a real sense of achievement.*

EQUIPMENT

Ski equipment provides the tools you need for fun and enjoyment on the slopes, and today's ski hardware is produced to a very high standard. The high-tech designs of the skis take into account such things as 'torsional rigidity', 'vibration dampening' and 'flex patterns'. However, these will probably be the last things on your mind when you are learning to ski! Skis recommended for beginners are normally easy turning ones, which have very forgiving characteristics.

The length of your skis should be just above head height, but no longer. Ski lengths are normally referred to in centimetres, ie '180s' are 180 centimetres (70 inches) long. If you rent skis, ensure that the soles are in good condition and that the edges are intact. Your feet are secured to the skis by bindings, which are required to hold you firmly to the skis yet release you when put under undue strain. Clearly this is a vital job, and they must be adjusted correctly to work properly, so make sure that the bindings are set correctly for your weight, age and ability when you are being kitted up.

The boots should be as comfortable as possible, fitting snugly around the foot and especially about the heel area. A loose fit will cause blisters and bad control when skiing.

Ski poles can feel very clumsy at first, but do not be put off. They are needed for balance, timing (see page 58) and also to assist in getting to the beginners' slope.

LEFT: *Ski poles are made of an aluminium shaft, on to which a steel ice tip is fixed to grip the snow. A small plastic roundel, or basket, is fitted to stop the pole sinking into the snow, and a 'grip' or handle incorporates a strap.*

BELOW: *There are many different types of skis on the market, but all incorporate steel edges. The ski bases are made of a plastic material which has a low friction co-efficient, helping the ski to glide over the snow.*

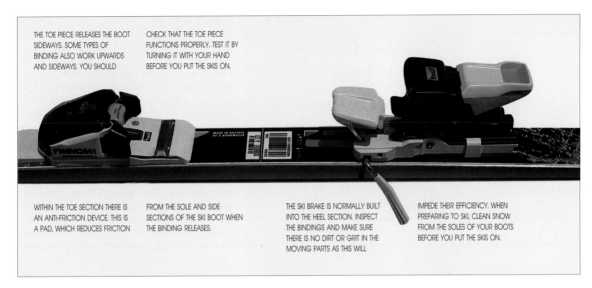

THE TOE PIECE RELEASES THE BOOT SIDEWAYS. SOME TYPES OF BINDING ALSO WORK UPWARDS AND SIDEWAYS. YOU SHOULD

CHECK THAT THE TOE PIECE FUNCTIONS PROPERLY. TEST IT BY TURNING IT WITH YOUR HAND BEFORE YOU PUT THE SKIS ON.

WITHIN THE TOE SECTION THERE IS AN ANTI-FRICTION DEVICE. THIS IS A PAD, WHICH REDUCES FRICTION

FROM THE SOLE AND SIDE SECTIONS OF THE SKI BOOT WHEN THE BINDING RELEASES.

THE SKI BRAKE IS NORMALLY BUILT INTO THE HEEL SECTION. INSPECT THE BINDINGS AND MAKE SURE THERE IS NO DIRT OR GRIT IN THE MOVING PARTS AS THIS WILL

IMPEDE THEIR EFFICIENCY. WHEN PREPARING TO SKI, CLEAN SNOW FROM THE SOLES OF YOUR BOOTS BEFORE YOU PUT THE SKIS ON.

Ski bindings

Ski bindings have the difficult and important job of keeping you attached to your skis. They should release you under excess stress or strain, protecting you from injury. Bindings comprise two sections: toe and heel pieces. In each part is a spring device, which holds the skier on to the skis. This spring must be adjusted according to the skier's weight, age and ski ability (this information is supplied in a Din table, which comes with the ski binding).

The ski brake is an integral part of the binding system built into the heel section. The brake is not designed to stop you! It is there to stop the ski sliding down the mountain if the bindings release. Without this the skis could career on and be a potential hazard. Always check that the bindings have an integral brake.

ABOVE: *All ski bindings come with a 'Din' table for adjusting to the correct setting according to weight, age and ski ability. If you are renting skis be sure that the table used is the right one for the binding.*

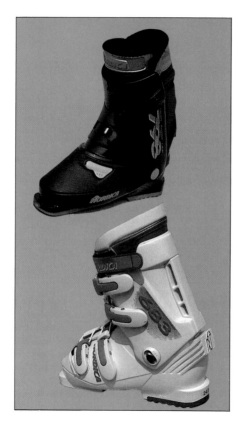

RIGHT, TOP: *With the rear-entry boot, there is usually only one clip to adjust. You are likely to come across it more often than the front-entry type as it is the most common type of ski boot used for hire purposes. The boot is simple to use and it is relatively easy to put on and take off. At the end of the day it is reassuring to know that undoing one clip and simply pulling the heel piece away releases your feet.*

RIGHT, BOTTOM: *The front-entry ski boot has clips across the top which secure you tightly. Its advantage is that each clip can be adjusted individually, refining the fit. The drawback is that taking these boots on and off can be fiddly and time-consuming.*

CLOTHING

Your ski clothing plays a vital role in keeping you comfortable at high altitudes. Many different types of insulation materials are used which combine warmth with lightness and flexibility. The best way to retain body warmth is to wear many thin layers rather than one thick one, because warm air is trapped between the layers. Thermal underwear can also help to retain body heat.

Protection from water also requires attention. Apart from the possibility of rain , it pays to remember that snow can be wet if you happen to fall on it! Your outer clothing does not have to be waterproof, but if it is, you will certainly feel the benefit. Many companies manufacture clothing that includes a waterproof membrane allowing the body to breath. Carefully inspect ski clothing such as ski jackets and salopettes for these qualities when you are buying them. Do not pretend that a pair of old walking or fishing socks will do the job of proper ski socks: they won't. Any wide knitted sock will be very uncomfortable when buckled in a ski boot.

Finally, eyes require above average protection when skiing, because of the altitude you are at, the exposure to the sun's rays and the glare from the snow's surface.

ABOVE: *Your ski clothing should be comfortable and durable to withstand mountain weather conditions. You will need to ensure that it is also flexible as skiing involves many body movements. Pockets are a very useful feature for carrying your sun cream and other necessities.*

ABOVE: *Ensure your ski jacket and trousers are properly insulated. Choose a suit with plenty of pockets, as these are useful on the mountain.*

Choose gloves with a good cuff that covers your wrists. Always opt for top-quality eye protection when buying sunglasses or goggles.

Bright colours are not just for the fashion conscious: they also help make sure you can be seen clearly in bad weather conditions.

UP AND DOWN THE SLOPE

BELOW: *Your first day on the mountain; if you get in a relaxed frame of mind, enjoying the scenery, you will learn more easily.*

Your first day on the beginners' slope will be filled with many thoughts (a common one being 'How do I stop?'). Providing you take skiing one stage at a time, learning will be easy, but never try something that you feel is beyond your ability. This world of slipping and sliding in all directions can, for some, be very disconcerting. You are no longer in the familiar world of grip, but now you have to make new and unfamiliar body movements to achieve simple things such as changing direction and stopping where you want to!

Warm-up exercises

AT LAST THE SNOW!

Now you are on the snow at last, the first thing to do is to put your skis on! This is much easier if you make sure that there is no snow on the soles of your boots. Snow on the soles will impede the binding's function, and could stop you getting the skis on altogether! The best way to remove the snow is to steady yourself using the ski poles and then lift up your foot to scrape off the snow with your hand. Giving the boot sole a gentle 'tap' with the ski pole will also help.

Warming up before you start each session, even after coffee or lunch breaks, helps prevent muscle strain and improves flexibility. Go through a routine to stretch and tone up the skiing muscles. Stretch gently and never 'bounce' to go that bit further. Slow movements are best. Walking on the flat is the first time you 'get mobile' in skis. Forget the normal way of walking, lifting one foot and then the other; now you must slide them along one at a time. When turning, be careful not to cross your skis, turn slowly and carefully, accurately thinking of the next move all the time.

LEFT: *It pays to warm up and stretch before you ski. Find a clear space away from other skiers.*

Keep stretches slow and gentle, and do not bounce as this can tear tendons.

WALKING ON THE FLAT

Your first movement on skis is walking: use it as an exercise to improve your balance. You need a flat area on which to try your first steps – all good ski resorts have a beginners' slope. If there has been a fresh fall of snow it may be necessary to wax the skis as new snow can stick to the ski bases: check with your rental company or tour representative.

LEFT: *Slide one ski in front of the other, keeping them parallel and making sure that they move in a straight line and do not converge or diverge as this will cause problems. If you go wrong here, you could cross the skis or even do the splits! The movement is simple – when you are walking, natural rhythm and balance dictate that you project the left foot so the right arm will swing forward. It is the same here, alternate arm and leg movements, using the poles to help propulsion and aid balance. The next stage is turning round at the end of your walk. Small steps are the key. Turn the feet alternately, taking care not to cross the skis either in front of you or, especially, at the tails.*

GETTING UP THE SLOPE

BELOW: *Stand with your skis across the slope. Bend your knees and tilt your skis on to their uphill edges. Then step sideways to gain height. Keep the skis apart by the width of your hips.*

By now you have experienced wearing skis while walking on a flat surface. Shifting from this controlled plane to an incline is a new challenge. Getting up the slope can be a tricky business if not tackled properly. To make life easier for yourself, keep relaxed and never rush. Keep your arms away from the body, your skis at hip width apart, and adopt a soft, rounded posture. This will keep you balanced and will make the climb much easier.

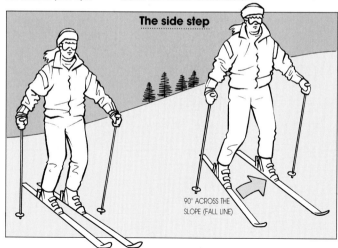

The side step

90° ACROSS THE SLOPE (FALL LINE)

14

ABOVE: *Keep your skis on their edges to support yourself. Step a comfortable distance* *sideways, and do not be tempted to take large steps. The knees are tilted towards the slope.*

The side step

The side step is probably the most popular method of getting yourself higher up the slope, the other method being the 'herringbone' (described on the right). Imagine standing on a flight of stairs which you are unable to climb in the normal way and are forced to ascend sideways. You would probably lift the leg closest to the stairs first and then bring the other one up to meet it. The movement is the same in side stepping. If the skis were to point directly up the slope they would obviously simply slide back down again, as they would present no resistance to the snow.

This is where the ski edges come in very useful. Simply stand at right angles to the slope keeping the skis across the hill. At this point you are 90 degrees to the line of least resistance. This line is known as the fall line. Before you try and walk up, be aware of the skis and the angle at which they are on the snow. They should be flat. Try rolling your knees into the hill and watch the ski edges make a platform in the snow. In doing this you are in effect making a staircase of your own to walk up. Once you are familiar with the feeling of applying the ski edges, try taking a few steps sideways and so upwards. Keep sideways to the fall line. Use your poles to help with balance. Try not to use them to push you up the slope.

The herringbone

The other popular way of getting yourself up the slope is using the herringbone method. This gets its name from the pattern that is left in the snow after the skier has walked up: the skis leave an imprint in the snow which resembles the skeleton of a herring. With this method you walk facing straight towards the slope, presenting the inside edges to the snow in order to provide enough resistance to stop sliding back down the hill. Some first-time skiers find this method easier, though you have to be careful not to catch the skis at the tails.

BELOW LEFT: *Notice the pattern left in the snow and the angle that the skis are to the slope. It can be easy to catch the skis at the tails, as you can see from the position of the right ski which is to be raised up and over the left one. The rear ski must be raised high for clearance.*

BELOW: *Notice that the weight is forward to maintain pressure on the ski edges. This in turn improves grip.*

TURNING INTO THE FALL LINE

Once you have reached the desired height you must turn into the fall line in order to position yourself to slide straight down the slope. Never rush this movement: take your time and think methodically. Following this simple method makes turning easy.

Step into a 'wedge' position using your poles for support. Keep the skis across the slope and turn the upper part of the body to face down hill. Extend both arms below you, pointing the pole tips down the slope, and reaching as far as is comfortable. Now position the pole tips in the snow either side of your ski boots and directly below your body.

One useful tip is to keep the arms straight when supporting yourself, as this rigidity helps to hold your weight. Turn the legs beneath your body, taking small steps. It might help to imagine that your skis are the slowly moving hands on a clock face. Keep turning until the ski tips are facing directly down the slope. Hold this position until you are ready to go.

Turning into the fall line

GETTING UP AFTER A FALL

If you fall you will need to be able to get up by yourself. Do not immediately struggle to get back on your feet; sit there for a few seconds to gather your thoughts. Start by making sure that your body is 'above' your skis, i.e. up the hill. From here turn the skis across the slope so that they are at 90 degrees to the fall line. Tuck the feet in as close as you can to the body. Using the poles to assist the rise, put them both together and place the tips in the snow close to your uppermost hip. Place one hand on top of the poles while the other holds them near the hip. Now simply pull with the top hand and push with the other. Ensure that you 'rock' forwards to maintain your centre of balance over the skis as this will assist the rise and so place you in the correct position when you stand up.

FAR LEFT: *After a fall, take a little time to gather your thoughts, then place your skis across the fall line and tuck your feet in close to the hips. Now prepare yourself to get the poles in position so that you can get up safely.*

TOP LEFT: *Make sure that the poles are tucked in close to the uppermost hip and that they are secure. Hold them near the bottom with one hand and place the other on top of the handles.*

BELOW LEFT: *As you rise up by pulling the poles with your top hand, and pushing with the bottom one, 'rock' your body forwards over your feet. This will make the rise easier as your body weight will be centred.*

17

DAY/1

RIGHT: *Seen from the side, your profile should be like the letter 'S', flexing at all the skiing joints: ankles, knees, hips and back. The ankles are flexed in the boots, keeping the weight centrally placed over the feet. Bend the knees slightly to allow the body to sit comfortably over the hips. Round your back and let the arms hang from the shoulders.*

FAR RIGHT: *Place the skis at hip width apart to form a stable base. The arms should be away from the body. Keep the pole tips behind you at all times. This basic skiing posture will remain with you throughout your skiing career.*

18

POSTURE

Your skiing posture is your key to success on the slopes. To ski efficiently and effectively, you must have a relaxed posture and well-balanced position. Try to create the shape of the letter 'S' with your body, for this will allow flexibility. Beginners are often advised to 'lean forwards', but this does not normally put the skier in the correct position at all. You do not ski by leaning forwards. What is meant is that you should keep your body over the skis in a central position. The advice probably stems from the novice's tendency to let the skis go ahead of the body and then over-compensate for leaning back. Providing that you are anticipating this movement there is no reason to lean forwards or backwards at all. Always keep your hands in front of you and away from your body to maintain good balance. However, do not force this position as the arms should be relaxed. Throughout this learning stage, keep the skis at hip width, as this will help to provide a stable platform for all basic manoeuvres.

STRAIGHT RUNNING

Straight running is your first sensation of sliding freely. To straight run, or 'shuss', as it is often called, find a nursery slope with a 'run out' to bring you to a gentle halt at the end of the exercise. Climb a few feet up the slope, and position yourself as for side stepping, with the skis parallel and facing directly down the fall line. Flex all the skiing joints and then allow yourself to slide down the hill. Go with the skis and don't be tempted to sit back, or try to walk.

BELOW LEFT: *This is an exercise to encourage independent leg action. As you straight run, imagine you are running on the spot, and start to lift your skis alternately. Raise the skis off the ground by lifting the knee up, not by leaning with the body. Keep the arms out for balance.*

BELOW: *Sliding the feet forward and back while straight running will build your awareness of dynamic balance. Make sure that you keep the weight evenly distributed on each ski. Staying low and keeping the arms away from the body assists in maintaining good balance.*

First steps

○ Begin a programme of exercises for flexibility, stamina and aerobic fitness ahead of your skiing trip.

○ Find good-quality clothing, remembering eye and skin protection.

○ Carry out warm-up exercises before you start skiing.

○ When attempting to side step up the hill, stay sideways to the slope, keeping your knees tilted into it.

○ If you fall, manoeuvre your skis across the slope so that you do not continue to slide when getting up.

○ When straight running, keep relaxed and stand over your feet, arms extended away from you. Do not lean backwards.

Straight running exercises

LIFT THE KNEE UP

SLIDE THE FEET
FORWARD AND BACK

THE SNOWPLOUGH

BELOW: *Snowploughing is a great confidence builder. Freedom on skis starts here. It is also a useful position to adopt if confronted with narrow tracks or difficult snow conditions.*

The snowplough is the foundation from which you will learn many ski techniques. It is your first technique of control, for deciding where and when you stop, or turn, for example. Once you learn it, you can move at will around the mountain.

Do not feel that snowploughing is purely for beginners: it is also a very useful way to learn about more advanced techniques. It involves, as the name suggests, ploughing the snow out of the way with the skis in a wedge position. The resistance made on the ski bases controls your speed and direction. Keep a good posture throughout and do not twist or contort the body. Stay relaxed and focus your mind on using the legs and feet.

THE PLOUGH GLIDE

In order to master the snowplough, you must first learn to glide. As with the straight run, look for a gentle slope with a sufficient amount of run-out area. Before you attempt to try this on the move it would help if you begin by putting the skis in a plough position on a flat surface. This helps in your awareness of the angle at which the skis need to be. Stand in a level area, then point the ski tips inwards and the tails out. (Sometimes this is referred to as a wedge position.) Flex your ankles in your boots and feel the edges of the skis pressing against the snow. After you have tried this a few times try hopping to bring the skis back to parallel.

ABOVE: *A braking plough is wider to produce more resistance, which slows the skier down.*

ABOVE: *When gliding, the plough is narrower and the body higher. Flatter skis give less resistance.*

Gliding on the move

When you feel confident and wish to attempt the glide on the move, side step up to comfortable height and turn around, positioning yourself in the fall line. Step the skis out into a narrow plough and, when you feel ready, start the glide. In this dynamic position keep the body over the skis and in an upright posture. Imagine that your skis are spreading the snow away from you. Indeed, the word spread describes very well the feeling you should get from the skis at this time. It is important that the pressure is maintained under the feet while gliding as this will control the speed of descent. Note that the edges only need to press inwards enough to create a little resistance. Too much edge will prevent the skis from spreading. It may feel as if the knees are bent inwards, because of the angle of the thigh in relation to the ball and socket joint in your hip. However, the knee does not bend inwards, just forwards to control the degree of edge required.

Always look ahead; looking down at your feet will cause unwanted tension and anxiety. It is important that you master the plough glide and that you feel comfortable while moving in this dynamic position, as all movements from now on in the snowplough will be taken from the glide position. You never waste time by practising plough movements.

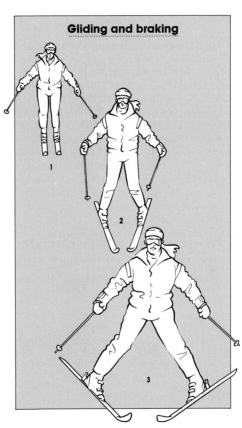

Gliding and braking

1

2

3

1 Rather than starting in the plough, try straight running first. When you feel ready, extend the legs to a wedge, feeling the difference between straight running and plough gliding.

2 As you extend, push the legs away while turning the tips inwards. Take care not to turn them too far and risk crossing the tips. The pressure is over the centre of the feet, not over the heels or toes.

3 A wider plough will slow your speed down considerably. The steeper the slope, the wider your plough will need to be. Sink down at this stage and keep pressure on the soles of the skis, otherwise they will return to a parallel position.

DAY/2

BELOW CENTRE: *The angle of the skis when in a glide. There is very little resistance to the snow, but enough to contain the speed. Create too much angle and the edges will cut into the snow and track, resulting in a cross at the ski tips.*

BELOW RIGHT: *When braking, more pressure is built up, so the angle of the skis needs to be more acute. The momentum which has been built up within you will be enough to stop the skis from tracking and so crossing. This is where the feeling of spreading is felt most. The legs have turned more, presenting more of the ski to the snow.*

PLOUGH BRAKING

Now that you have mastered the glide and started to gain some control over the speed at which you travel down the slope, the next (and crucial!) skill to work on is stopping. Plough braking is simply a wider gliding plough. More resistance is required to reduce the momentum which has built up from the glide down the fall line. Applying more of an acute angle on the ski edges against the snow surface is the obvious answer, but this is not enough on its own because it could have an effect elsewhere on the body and disrupt your balance. However, if you follow these simple instructions, you will find that the braking is easy.

There are two main ways in which to brake: either sink down with the legs and spread the skis apart, or stay in a low position and extend the legs away from the body. Both ways will have the effect of creating more pressure against your line of travel. When sinking, simply use your body weight to spread the skis wider. When extending, use your leg muscles to push the skis away. In both methods, it is also important to turn the legs so that the tips of the skis are pointing slightly inwards, keeping the weight evenly distributed over the whole foot.

Occasionally you might discover you have a tendency to sit back when braking. This is quite common, but doing this will only encourage the skis to want to return to parallel, and as a result you will go faster – the opposite of what you want to achieve. Focus your mind on pushing the feet away and creating more resistance against the snow. Using the muscles in your legs, rather than the framework of your skeleton, will give you more control when braking.

22

ABOVE: *Note the good posture and flexed position of the body during braking. Maintaining this position keeps the weight over the feet. The arms are symmetrical and at equal distances from the body. If the plough is not symmetrical and the body is twisted, the tendency is to veer off your line and so lose control. It is important here that you apply the pressure to the skis by pressing on your feet, and not just spreading the skis into a very wide plough. You must achieve a combination.*

2 SNOWPLOUGH GLIDE

1

SNOWPLOUGH BRAKE

1 *Note that the knee and ankle are flexed when braking, whereas in a plough glide the knees are not bent so much. As you brake, 'round' the body to stay relaxed and ensure that the pressure is distributed over the centre of the skis.*

2 *Here you can see that the stance for the glide is higher, while the skis are kept in a narrower plough. Note that the body still has a rounded position, showing the good flexibility required to cope with undulations in the terrain covered.*

The snowplough

○ *Stay in a good posture throughout – do not contort your body.*
○ *Look ahead at all times, and do not look down at your feet, as this will cause tension.*
○ *In a gliding plough, keep the skis in a narrow plough with little edge, which minimizes resistance.*
○ *When braking, feel the resistance build up under the feet. Simply spreading the skis out is not enough.*
○ *Resist any temptation to sit back during braking.*
○ *When gliding and braking down the fall line, ensure that the arms and skis are kept symmetrical at all times.*

RIGHT: The T-bar and (FAR RIGHT) chair lifts. The T-bar lift is a sociable mode of transport, and providing you and your partner keep equal pressure on both feet, the journey is easy. On lifts such as this it is important that you do not sit down; simply rest on the bar and allow it to pull you along. Before you get on a T-bar lift, make sure that your ski poles are in one hand so that the other hand is free to grab hold of the bar. Keep the skis parallel and pointing up the slope – do not be tempted to snowplough. When dismounting, make sure that you are clear of other skiers when you let go of the bar.

SKI LIFTS

Now that you have spent some time on snow ploughing you are ready to take the ski lift to your next challenge. Types of lift vary between different countries and resorts.

The T-bar lift

Many Austrian resorts use a T-bar lift. Although designed for two people, one person can use it quite safely.

The T-bar lift

The chair lift

There are many different types of chair lift, from single seaters to express four and six seaters. When using any chair lift be sure to remove your hands from the straps of your ski poles. Hold the poles in one hand, keeping the other free to help you get on and off the chair. The skis must be kept parallel and pointing up the slope. Always pull the safety barrier down. When dismounting always ski clear of the lift and away from other users.

Button lifts

As with chair lifts, there are different kinds of button lifts: the rigid type and the cord to spring box type. When using either of these, do not sit down on them; rather, keep your weight on your feet and simply let the button pull you up the slope. When using the spring box type you must pull the button down from the hanger to start whereas the rigid type is already at waist height. There should be an attendant to assist you on the beginners' slope lift.

Other types

In addition to the lifts mentioned here, there are many other forms of uphill transport at ski resorts. Some resorts have invested heavily in very modern, state-of-the-art equipment which allows thousands of people to be transported up the mountain every hour. For example the cabin type of lift takes anything from two to forty people in one go. Cable cars are used in some areas where skiers need to be transported to great heights.

LEFT AND FAR LEFT: A 'rigid pole' type button lift. Prepare yourself while approaching the departure point. Make sure that your poles are in one hand, leaving the other free to grab the button. Ensure that your skis are facing up the hill and are parallel. Take the button and pull it down between your legs. Remember, do not actually sit on it, but, rather, simply let the lift pull you up the slope. Once you are on the move, keep the skis parallel throughout and do not attempt to snowplough. With the skis pointing straight up the slope be sure to stick to the tow track as indicated. At the top of the lift simply take the button away from between your legs and let it go. Do not 'throw' it.

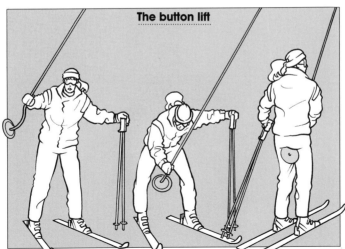

The button lift

CHANGING DIRECTION

BELOW: *Turning is all about feeling the forces of nature and using them to your advantage. Snowplough turns are your introduction to this exciting world.*

S nowplough turns will enable you to steer yourself in the direction you wish. This will involve experiencing the feeling of moving out of the fall line. Turning on skis is not the same as turning the body in a desired direction as you would without skis. Now you must learn a new way of changing direction by using more pressure on one ski than the other. For example to turn to the right the pressure will need to be on the left ski and vice versa. These are the fundamentals, but there are other factors to take into consideration.

LEFT: *The ability to turn will give you the freedom to experience otherwise unreachable areas. When turning in a snowplough, keep the posture relaxed. As you pressurize the ski you will start to travel in the direction in which the ski is pointing. This will take you out of the fall line, but your momentum will pull you in the original direction. To compensate for this, and to complete the turn, you must allow the body to flex over the turning ski.*

The plough turn

CENTRAL POSITION
IN THE FALL LINE

1

2

3

4

PRESSURE HERE

1 *From a plough glide press with the right hand on the right knee. This will start to pressurize the ski. Note that as you sink down to press and go round the turn, what is now the 'top' ski is slightly in front of the lower one.*

2 *After completing one turn return to a central position. At this early stage it is best to stop and be clear in your mind of the next steps for a turn the opposite way.*

3 *Now try a turn to the left. As before, place the hand on the knee. Note that in these turns the knee and ankle are flexed, applying pressure down to the turning ski (shown in **4**). Your changes of direction will be crude at first, and we will work on skills to improve on this.*

27

BELOW RIGHT: *From a plough glide, apply more edge to one ski. This will cause you to travel sideways across the slope while still facing down the fall line. Do not attempt to turn and change direction. Staying low over the feet will help you in applying the edge. Look ahead and fix your eyes on something directly in front of you. When one ski has been edged, ensure that the other one is almost flat so that it is not resisting the direction of travel. Keep your arms out and away from the body, and symmetrical. Repeat the exercise, practising the turn in the other direction (see far right).*

EDGE AWARENESS

Your ski edges are instruments of control, and using them correctly is an important part of skiing technique. The edges run the entire length of the ski and should be relatively sharp, though this is less important for soft fresh snow. To become more aware of what the edges do it is a good idea to try some exercises to feel the reaction of certain movements. For example, imagine the sideways walk of a crab. The following exercise mimics that movement; you are not turning but simply moving diagonally across the slope. Note that this exercise involves using more edge on one ski than the other. Your snowplough turns will benefit from this technique, for the 'edge work', combined with pressure and leg turning, will help you start to produce more polished and efficient and 'rounder' turns.

Working with the edges

In order to apply the edge of the ski accurately, you must be aware of your body movements and their effects. You may feel as if the knee is rolling inwards, but this is not happening. The knee operates in a forward direction and not sideways. The increased angle of the skis to the snow is produced by the thigh rolling in the hip socket. In order to get the feel of this movement, try the following exercise. Sit on a high stool, and let your legs hang over the seat, so the knees are bent. Now pull your right foot sideways and upwards so you can see the outer edge of the shoe. Notice that the right knee looks as if it goes inwards. Now place your hand on your thigh and feel it roll. The only place for it to roll is from the hip. Try swinging both legs from left to right, focusing your attention on the movements. Provided you keep the hips facing down the hill and do not twist them, applying more edge to one ski will be easy. Returning to the movement in the high stool exercise, some people find this movement easier if they think of flattening one ski rather than edging the other. This will of course have the same effect. Practise this for an hour or two before you go back to attempting a snowplough turn. The resulting blend of edge and pressure will assist in the change of direction. Be careful not to over-emphasize either of these ingredients.

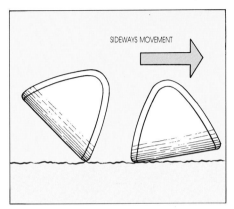

SIDEWAYS MOVEMENT

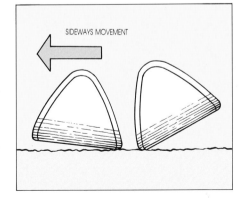

SIDEWAYS MOVEMENT

LEFT: *Note the angle of the skis to the snow's surface during edging for a right and left turn. As one ski is tilted the snow will build up underneath it, increasing the resistance and deflecting you in the opposite direction. As long as the other ski is flatter, the deflected movement will easily propel you across the slope. It should be noted, however, that the non-resisting ski still requires a very slight inward tilt so that it does not catch the outside edge while moving sideways. You may feel that turning in one direction is easier than the other; this is quite common. Perseverance will win the day! Make these movements slowly, to give yourself enough time to think.*

DAY/3

LINKING THE TURNS

BELOW: *The central position in the fall line is the key to linking turns; it is from here you transfer the weight. Note that the stance is high next to the pole and low after it.*

Now that you have mastered turning in both directions, your next target is to link your turns together. There is a tendency after finishing one turn to twist or turn the body in the opposite direction. If you do this the result will probably not be a turn at all, for you are more likely to find yourself still travelling in the original direction. The reason for this is the lack of weight transference from one ski to the other.

Your first efforts at linking turns should be to try two turns only. As with all new techniques, start off in small amounts and build up. From the fall line, in a gliding plough, start the first turn. As you sink into the turn slowly count from one to four while pressurizing the turning ski. This will make the turn progressive. When the turn loses its momentum and is far enough round, start rising up from the legs and stand high. The pressure that was on the turning ski should now be distributed evenly on both skis. This will turn you into the fall line. The crucial point is to be central and standing high in the fall line, and pausing in this position will get you ready for the start of the next turn. Be careful to resist the temptation to rotate the hips to the direction requires. Rather, the change of pressure and increase of edge on the new turning ski will take you round quite naturally.

Teaching aids such as ski poles stuck in the snow as markers for turning points will give you targets to go round. Make it fun, and treat it like a miniature slalom course. You can also use them as prompters; in other words, when you are in line with the pole ahead of you, you should be in a low position and turning, whereas by the time that you are parallel with the pole, you should be in a high position and in the fall line. Looking ahead at all times and reading the terrain helps you think ahead.

Linking the turns

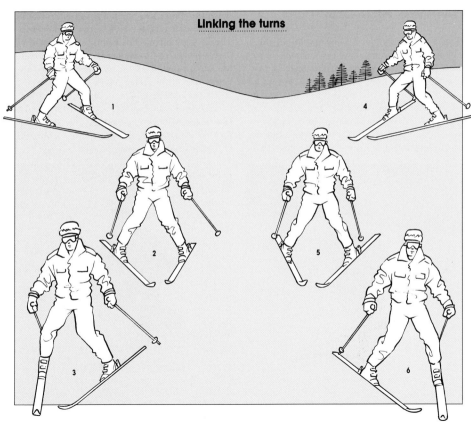

LEFT: *As pressure is placed on the lower turning ski, and the direction is across the fall line, the top ski will be slightly ahead of the lower* **1**. *This will help keep the body facing the direction of travel and not twisted up the slope* **2**. *As you press and edge the lower ski, try actively advancing the top ski, making sure that you do this from the hip and not just the foot and leg* **3**. *Rise and extend the legs to establish a central position in the fall line. This will tend to flatten the skis and so release the edge grip, leaving you free to slide into the fall line* **4**. *Stand high and do not rush into the next turn* **5**. *When you feel comfortable, start the next turn. Note how the top ski is advanced* **6**.

FLOWING AND RESISTING

Good skiing is all about flowing and resisting. The skill of combining these two elements determines the quality of movement that is produced. Gravity, one of the great forces of nature, is the source of power in skiing, and its force can be harnessed by the good skier, using it to work the skis to his or her advantage.

As you ski, you gain momentum, and the energy produced from your body mass flows down the slope. Too much flowing will result in your travelling faster and faster, and eventually losing control. So learning to resist that flow is crucial to staying in command. However, too much resist also has unwanted results – the worst obviously being no movement at all! Using both skills in their correct proportions will produce rounded, smooth turns. Your aim is to harness the flow and control the resistance, to help make your skiing virtually effortless and allow nature to work for you.

BELOW RIGHT: *Feel the difference when you apply more edge in a turn: the ski grips and probably stops (FAR RIGHT). This is resisting. Now glide in a plough down the fall line (NEAR RIGHT). This is flowing. Note the skiers in these two pictures. They are both flowing and resisting, but in different amounts. Too much resisting can show up by snow spraying up at the end of a turn from under the skis. A good mixture of the two will result in smooth flowing arcs. While practising your plough turns, try to feel the flow and resist as you change direction and experiment with varying amounts.*

Experimenting with flow and resist

Plough turns are an ideal way to experiment with flow and resist. From a plough glide try increasing the amount of edge, pressure and width of plough to control the momentum. As you become more aware of the sensation, notice the different results as you vary the pressure and edge in a plough turn. On the beginners' slope, explore ways of harnessing momentum in your turns. Try to stay relaxed, and feel the effects of your movements on your upper body.

BELOW LEFT: *Flow down the fall line in a gliding plough. Feel momentum building up, but do not brake and stop. Rather, count slowly from one to four before you attempt to resist. Keep the skis equally weighted so that you continue to glide in a straight line.*

BELOW: *To resist, start by making your plough turn. As the skis turn out of the fall line, feel the momentum start to reduce. The ski with the pressure and edge on it will resist against your line of travel (the fall line) and so deflect you in the desired direction.*

Changing direction

○ When turning in the snowplough, keep the posture relaxed. As you pressurize the ski you will start to travel in the direction in which the ski is pointing.

○ After completing one turn always return to a central position.

○ In turns, the knee and ankle are flexed, applying pressure to the turning ski.

○ When one ski has been edged, keep the other almost flat to prevent it resisting the direction of travel.

○ Staying low over the feet will help you in applying the edge.

○ Using flow and resist in their correct proportions will help you to produce smooth turns.

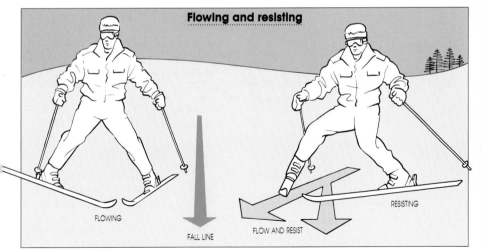

Flowing and resisting

FLOWING

FALL LINE

FLOW AND RESIST

RESISTING

OUT AND ABOUT

With your new skills of mobility, you are free to enjoy the adventure of discovering new slopes and new areas to ski. This sense of independence is one of the great joys of the sport. The lift station or tourist office at your ski resort will have a map of the skiing area to guide you around the mountain. These maps, however, are not usually terribly accurate, and are produced as a guide only. The maps are normally in full colour, and should be studied carefully before you decide on the most appropriate slopes to visit.

WHICH SLOPES?

Ski runs in most resorts are graded by either the colour of the piste markers or sometimes name only. Ascertain from the piste map which colour or name shows the easiest runs, and attempt this kind first. Check that connecting runs returning to the beginners' slope are equally easy. The black run seems to be the one that every skier wants to go down. May be they can get down it, but are they in control? Do not be tempted to try slopes that are graded as difficult.

LEFT: *Always follow the piste markers and never stray off the track. Normally the markers are numbered, starting at the top with the highest and so decreasing as you descend. Stick to easy runs at first.*

Navigating in the mountains with a resort map on a fine day can be good fun and very rewarding. However, these maps are not intended for mountaineering or venturing off the piste. They are for guidance only and for showing connecting lifts, etc. The map will show the different types of lifts that connect one run with another. Heights and names of mountains will also be included. Check that you are familiar with the location of first aid posts; they are usually at the top or bottom of the main lift stations. You should not, of course, be venturing up the hill for the first time without a guide or your instructor. If you're planning your first venture and the weather is bad, don't go – play safe and leave the mountain for a fine day.

35

TRAVERSING

RIGHT: *As you stand in the traverse position, get yourself comfortable and slightly advance the top ski. Keep the feet at hip width apart and most of your weight on the lower ski. Note in the photograph that the ski has flexed as it rides over a slight dip in the snow. A slight outward leaning of the body while tilting the knees inwards will improve your edge awareness. Traversing is about skiing on the edges, therefore no sideways slippage should occur. Side slipping is a separate issue; it is useful in learning the feeling of sideways movement, allowing the edges to release their grip.*

Your main objective so far has been to get accustomed to the feel of sliding down the slope. Now we will look at 'traversing', or travelling across the slope. This involves moving across the fall line rather than directly down along it. Traversing can be used in linking snowplough turns together or, more commonly, in finding your way across the slope to the cafe! The manoeuvre does not entail the use of flow and resist to create a turn. It is basically a method of skiing in a parallel stance across the slope, and the ski edges play an important part here.

Stand with your skis facing diagonally across the slope, making sure that they are on their edges and form a good platform to hold you. Push yourself off and keep the skis on their edges as you travel diagonally. The stance is such that your body will be leaning slightly outwards while the knees are tilted inwards, keeping you balanced over the skis. Let the skis 'track' into the snow. The skis will tend to veer slightly up the slope; this is due to the ski shape and the grip of the edges. Most of your body weight should be on the lower ski. If you find that there is too much weight on the upper ski it is likely that you are 'banking' the body inwards. Correct this immediately, as it forms no part of a well balanced ski technique.

Traversing

DIRECTION OF TRAVEL

FALL LINE

ABOVE: *This skier shows a well-balanced position for traversing. Note that the top ski is slightly in front of the lower one; this allows the hips, and so the upper body, to face in the correct direction. The body should not face directly down the slope, this only 'twists' the body in an uncomfortable position. Facing the direction of travel is all that is required.*

SIDE SLIPPING

Treat the side slip here as an exercise, though it might come in handy if you wish to get down a steep slope where you are unable to turn in the normal way. Side slipping is a way of losing height without making turns. More importantly it will encourage you to use your legs when releasing or applying the ski edges.

LEFT, TOP: *Note here that the knees are 'tilted' inwards and so apply the ski edges into the snow. By 'tilting' the knees inwards you are making 'steps' for yourself in the snow to stand on.*

LEFT, BOTTOM: *When you 'roll' the knees out away from the slope, the skis will start to slide sideways, as they no longer hold an edge to support you. Be careful, however, not to 'roll' the knees out too far, as this will only succeed in catching the lower edge of the ski and so cause you to trip. It takes only slight movements in skiing to achieve a result. Experimenting with these different positions will give you valuable skills to use later on in your skiing career.*

37

DAY /4

RIGHT: *Side slipping in action. The manoeuvre exploits the fact that when the skis are at an angle to the slope they will grip the snow. The knees are tilting inwards here and so 'edging' the skis. As you roll the thigh (and so the knee) outwards and down the slope the edges will flatten slightly. As a result you will slip sideways. If you face in the direction in which you wish to travel and spread your weight over the length of the skis, you will move squarely down the slope. Too much weight over your heels, and your body will start to turn into the fall line. Weight on the toes will cause you to slide backwards.*

38

Direct side slipping

The value of side slipping is underestimated by many skiers, who regard it as a mere exercise. In fact, it plays a vital role in teaching the body to be aware of travelling in a sideways motion. As a great deal of skiing involves this movement you should practise side slipping regularly. There are two basic methods of side slipping: direct and diagonal. Start with direct slipping. From a side step position, face your upper body down the slope, with the tips of the poles behind you and the hands in front. Begin by flexing the body over the skis and tilting the knees inwards. If you were to view your body from the side it would resemble a 'C' shape or a half moon. Now rise slightly and rock the thighs (and therefore the knees) outwards, releasing the grip of the ski edges and starting the slip. Don't overexaggerate this movement, however, or you may catch the lower edge of the ski and trip up. As you move, keep facing in the direction of travel. It may be necessary to push with the ski pole tips in the snow behind you to initiate the movement. Sometimes in deeper fresh snow the build up of snow under the ski soles is so great that the push will be essential to clear the way. Shuffling the feet forwards and backwards also helps. When you want to stop, simply re-apply the edges by tilting the knees (and therefore the thighs) inwards.

Diagonal side slipping

Diagonal side slipping is more dynamic than the direct slip as there is some forward movement as well. From the traverse position, pointing at a fairly gradual angle, start moving across the slope. Flatten the skis, and you will travel diagonally but lose height from the original traverse direction. This requires more use of balance on your part so anticipate the outward leaning of the body in the direction of the slip. You may feel that you should lean away from the direction of travel. Resist the temptation – you will simply be allowing the skis to travel on while you fall into the slope!

Practise diagonal side slipping and play with varying amounts of edge and pressure as you go. As you slip, try applying more pressure by flexing the knees and ankles to increase the edge. It is likely that you will turn out of the diagonal and induce a 'swing' in a parallel position. It is important to try these swings from both sides and attempt them from increasingly steeper traverses. Always ensure that you have a clear area with a satisfactory run-out.

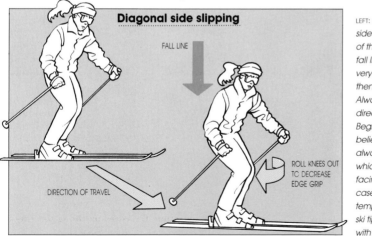

Diagonal side slipping

FALL LINE

ROLL KNEES OUT TC DECREASE EDGE GRIP

DIRECTION OF TRAVEL

LEFT: *During diagonal side slipping, be aware of the direction of the fall line. Begin by using a very shallow angle and then start to increase it. Always face in the direction of travel. Beginners often falsely believe that travel is always in the direction in which the ski tips are facing. This is not the case, so ignore the temptation to follow the ski tips, but rather, 'go with the flow'.*

Traversing/side slip

○ *When traversing, move diagonally across the slope, keeping the ski edges applied in the snow.*

○ *The knees are tilted inwards and body outwards while traversing, helping your balance. Weight is on the lower ski.*

○ *Traversing relies on 'edges' in the snow while side slipping relies on the ski base 'flat' on the snow.*

○ *During direct or diagonal side slipping the body faces the direction of travel and not the direction of the ski tips.*

39

GETTING BETTER

BELOW: *The parallel turn is a movement all good skiers need. There are many methods of doing it, and all involve leg turning.*

The exercises described so far have given you a grounding in some basic ingredients of good ski technique. These are the skills of applying pressure and edge in dynamic positions using momentum as the force. All are used in the next manoeuvre – the parallel turn –

when your skis remain parallel throughout. To progress to this from the plough turn with which you are already familiar, you need to develop the skill of turning the legs. One way to achieve this is by using the basic swing, which is half parallel and half gliding plough.

BASIC SWING

The two words say it all: basic, as in feet apart; swing, as in a parallel arc across the slope. You have already learnt the main ingredients of turning, and now must deal with leg turning. You could say that basic swings are half parallel and half a gliding plough. The movement has three key elements: 1 a gliding plough in the fall line; 2 turning one leg in the desired direction; 3 skidding the skis across the fall line into the new direction. The technique of skidding is covered more fully on page 44.

LEFT: *As you start to turn, let momentum pull you down the slope. The pressure built up on your lower ski will take the weight off the upper one, encouraging it to turn parallel.*

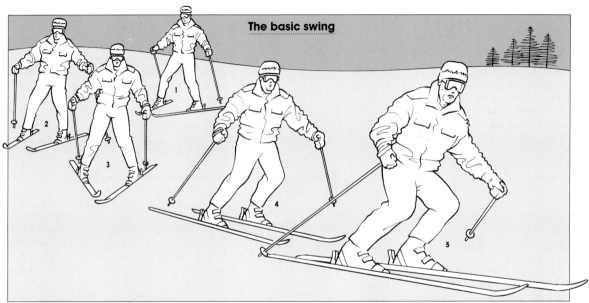

The basic swing

1 From the plough glide, stand high in the fall line, counting slowly from 1 to 4 to gain some momentum. Look ahead to anticipate where you will start the turn. Make sure the slope is clear.

2 Before you apply pressure on the ski, as you would in a plough turn, start to turn the left leg by turning the ski tip. Do not be tempted to pull it in close to the other ski.

3 As the ski starts to turn, you should begin to sink with the knees and ankles over the skis. Check that your body is facing in the direction of movement and is not twisted up the hill.

4 The skis will now be parallel. Remember to retain them in a wide stance. The turn will take the form of a skidding arc across the fall line. Note that the top ski is in front of the lower one.

5 At the end of the turn your stance should be quite low to compensate for the build up of pressure under the feet. Try these turns in both directions until you can achieve them easily.

RIGHT: *As you approach the fall line, look ahead to check there is a clear area for the turn. At this point you should be starting to rise up from the legs so that your stance is high when you get to the fall line. Stay like this for a short period before you start the turn. Keep the hands away from the body so that you maintain good, dynamic balance. Spread the skis into a narrow plough as you rise, and try not to step one ski out at a time as this will stop the flow and thus eliminate the swing at the end of the turn. Try to spread both skis evenly. At this point you can use the gliding plough to regain your momentum.*

Turning the leg

Your first attempts at basic swings may not feel as if they flow at all. This is not unusual. The point at which you turn your leg is the crucial element, and is often the area that requires the most work. It is wise to practise turning the leg on a flat area first. The tendency is to turn the hip with the leg, and this means that the whole body moves. To rectify this problem, stand with the skis in a narrow plough on a flat area. Supporting yourself with your poles, turn the tip of one ski outwards. Make sure that the knee and ankle are flexed to get the full effect from the movement. If they are not flexed, the result will be twisting at the hips. Do not fall into the trap of trying to bring one ski in close to the other. (This will have the same effect as did trying to remove the stabilizers from your first bicycle before you were ready – you will fall over!) Concentrate on keeping the skis at hip width apart as you turn them.

After a few attempts at this in a static position you are ready for the slope. From a comfortable height up the hill, start by standing in a narrow gliding plough facing diagonally across the slope (rather like a snowplough traverse). Try this first in the traverse position before you attempt it from the fall line, as it makes turning the leg easier. Proceed across the hill with most of your weight on the lower ski and gain some momentum. When the skis are flowing, start the turn by turning the uphill ski tip further across the slope. Note that when the upper ski is turned you should allow your body to sink over the skis, compensating for the momentum. Practise this a few times to feel the movement and then try it from the fall line. You must be very positive when attempting these turns, and keep looking straight down the hill.

Now you are ready to try linking these turns together. As with the snowplough linked turns, the basic formula of rising in the fall line and holding for a few seconds remains. The only difference is that you are now turning the leg to become parallel to the other ski.

LEFT: *Towards the end of the turn, when the skis are parallel, remember to check that they are at hip width apart, as this is important in maintaining your balance. At this point you will be much lower than you would be in the fall line. Compare this photograph to the one on page 42; see how much lower the posture is.*

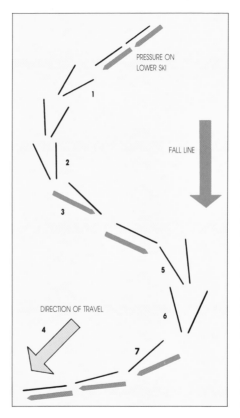

PRESSURE ON LOWER SKI

FALL LINE

DIRECTION OF TRAVEL

LEFT: *From the end of the turn, as you travel diagonally across the slope, the weight will be on your lower ski. At **1** start to rise and displace both skis. When you reach **2** the skis will be in a narrow gliding plough facing directly down the fall line. Between here and **3**, start to turn the inside leg towards the direction of your turn. During the sinking phase, gradually apply the pressure to the lower ski at **3**. The skis will now return to a parallel position. Note that **4** shows your actual direction of travel, which is a slight skid across the hill, not the direction in which your ski tips are facing (this is a common mistake). Repeat the manoeuvre in reverse for a turn in the opposite direction, as in **5** to **7**.*

43

DAY 5

44

SKIDDING

Skidding is a useful discipline which will improve your awareness of travelling sideways. Unlike slipping, skidding requires momentum. Try this exercise. Start in a steep traverse then, when you have gained momentum, turn both legs across the line of travel. At this point you can do one of three things: you can allow your body to carry on in the same line as momentum and launch yourself over the skis to face the consequences; you can avoid facing the line of travel and lean back up the slope, so falling inwards; or you can face your line of travel and so maintain momentum. The third option is the way to stay on your feet!

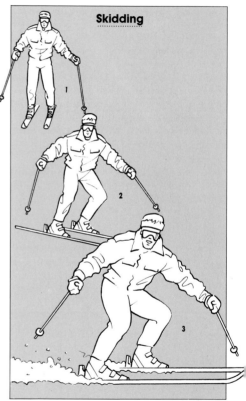

Skidding

LEFT: *As the ski edges increase their grip through the turn, so your momentum is trying to compensate by pulling you down the fall line. Your response should be to flex the upper body over the skis. Note that the skier on the left has very little angulation; on her relatively flat skis she will not have sufficient pressure or edge to make effective turns. The skier on the right, on the other hand, is using this invisible force to transfer the pressure to the ski edges by angulation, and so is prepared for the next turn.*

The basic swing

○ *Basic swings are half parallel and half a gliding plough.*

○ *The basic swing has three elements: gliding plough in the fall line; turning one leg in the desired direction; and skidding the skis across the fall line into the new direction.*

○ *As you start your plough turn, the pressure built up on your lower ski will take the weight off the upper one, encouraging it to turn parallel.*

○ *When leg turning, make sure that the knee and ankle are flexed to get the full effect.*

○ *Angulation is an outward leaning of the body with an inward tilt of the legs.*

Angulation

Angulation is an outward leaning of the body with an inward tilt of the legs which should occur naturally, and which helps you to stay in balance over your skis. It is part of any effective ski turn, and when it happens it makes your profile a 'C' shape. Effective angulation will only occur when there is sufficient momentum. If angulation is not achieved, the body leans into the slope and turns become lazy and inaccurate. The consequence is an over-reliance on the top ski, which prevents accurate steering and is known as banking. Banking can be fun but is not conducive to effective learning.

45

LETTING GO

BELOW: *Don't fight gravity and momentum, but let your skiing flow and use your skills with edges, pressure and turning to control your descent.*

Go with the flow is an appropriate phrase which applies here! The awareness of flowing and resisting as mentioned earlier (see page 32) is important to enable the skis to work for you. However, all too often skiers become anxious and tend to hold themselves back. The resulting failure to gain momentum means the skis function ineffectively. Find some new slopes with plenty of space to ski on and make sure that you really let yourself go. Keep a cool head and always plan ahead on how and where you are going to make the turns.

LEFT: *The forces of gravity and the effect of momentum can be clearly seen here. The skier has unleashed her power in a highly controlled way, and so can you. Provided that the skis are across the fall line, on their edges and have pressure on them, they will turn by themselves. Balancing these forces with the upper body and the inward tilt of your legs will flex the skis in a reverse camber to steer you across the slope.*

LEFT: *The skier on the left is apprehensive of turning and tense. His upper body is twisted up the slope, so his weight is not on the turning ski. In contrast, the skier behind him is sliding freely, standing well on his feet and letting the skis work.*

A   B

ABOVE: *Track A shows a rush to get out of the fall line and a long, inactive traverse; Track B shows rounded turns with little traverse: much better.*

ACTIVE TURNING

So far we have mainly talked about pressurizing the turning ski. There are, however, other approaches to turning. These alternatives can be split into two types of approaches: active turning, and passive turning. The following exercises can be used to refine and enhance your technique of turning. You may find that passive turning is the better approach for you as a beginner.

First, we should clarify the widely used expression 'pressurize the turning ski', which refers to active turning. This relies heavily on your commitment to the lower ski, which is pressurized (edged) to make it turn.

The pressure is enhanced by flexing the knees and ankles over your feet, bending the ski boot collar and so transferring the movement to the skis. Imagine that you are trying to press the ski into the snow. This will force the ski to bend into the reverse camber and therefore send you round in an arc corresponding to the arc of the flexed ski. Try turning by exerting maximum pressure over the ski (this is best attempted in a snowplough position the first few times you try). Remember to keep the pressure in the middle of the foot as you go round the turn. Some people find it easier to think in terms of pressing and steering the foot rather than the ski.

RIGHT, TOP: *Passive turning. Here, the skier is in a mid stance position, just before turning, ready to lighten the upper ski. Note that there is still some flex at the knees and ankles at this pre-turn stage.*

RIGHT, BOTTOM: *As you take the weight off your upper ski (but without actually lifting the foot), you will find that your lower leg takes the pressure and begins to turn automatically. This is a passive turn.*

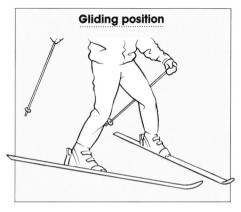

Gliding position

Turn preparation

RELEASE OF PRESSURE

PASSIVE TURNING

In contrast to active turns, passive turns require a very subtle approach, calling on you to use thought power rather than muscle action. The result will be the same as the active turn, but you will produce it in an effortless way. It is important here that you think of 'lightening up' the inside ski (rather than exerting pressure on the lower one), and that you adopt the idea of 'one thought, one action'.

BELOW: *From a gliding plough facing down the fall line, focus on making the inside ski very light – try lifting the knee very slightly upwards. The weight will then be transferred to the lower ski. This manoeuvre should be done in a low, mid-stance position.*

DAY/6

Passive turning

RIGHT: *When performed well, passive turns are effortless, allowing you to ski all day without undue tiredness. It is important however that you focus only on 'un-weighting' the top ski and do not think about exerting pressure on the lower one. As has been emphasized, the method requires a 'mind over matter' approach. After a few linked snowplough turns you will find that turning the inside leg to the parallel position becomes a natural and easy movement. Imagine that you are pedalling a bicycle, with your legs rising and sinking. These are the movements of the passive turn.*

1 *Think only of making the top ski as light as possible. It will help if you imagine that your inside ski is being pulled away from the ground.*

2 *As you start to turn, ensure that your upper body is angulated over the lower ski. If you lean into the hill, the weight will be on the upper ski and so make the turning lower ski inactive.*

3 *It may help if you point the top ski tip up slightly. This has the effect of bringing the body over the turning ski. When the turn is right, you will feel that you are being guided along like a train along a track.*

FEEL AND BALANCE

Most of 'Day 6' has been spent on investigating and improving your awareness of dynamic movements on skis. Hurrying from one technique to another without foundation training like this will not necessarily encourage progress, however. Just as important is to become familiar with the feel of skis and snow under your feet. Remember that the weight should be over the central part of the feet and not over the toes or heels. It is useful to spend time on finding out exactly where you are standing on your feet. Use the snowplough as the vehicle from which to investigate where you stand. Unclipping the boots will encourage you to take a central position over the skis. It is also important to focus your mind on the task in hand: one thought, one action.

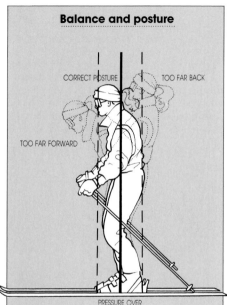

Balance and posture

CORRECT POSTURE

TOO FAR BACK

TOO FAR FORWARD

PRESSURE OVER
MIDDLE OF FOOT

LEFT: *Try a few turns with the boots unclipped. This will force you to stand centrally, although it may initially make you feel out of control.*

ABOVE: *The central figure here has the seat tucked in and body weight carried over the hips. In the other positions the weight is not centred.*

Active/passive turning

○ *Keep relaxed, and plan what you are going to do well ahead of each turn.*

○ *Let your skiing flow and use your skills with edges, pressure and turning to control your descent.*

○ *For parallel turns the skis must turn simultaneously.*

○ *For the direct method of plough to parallel, you must be punchy, rhythmic and positive in how you handle the skis.*

○ *The passive turn requires that you extend the legs, and not retract them under the body.*

○ *When turning the inside leg, be sure to lighten it by angulating over the lower ski.*

THE PARALLEL

BELOW: *There are many ways to get to the parallel turn from a snowplough. Try different approaches to find the one that suits you best.*

Most skiers aspire to being able to do the parallel turn. The basic parallel involves turning without any ploughing at all. The feet are at hip width apart and the ski edges change simultaneously. However, it is not all that different from the plough that you have been practising for the last few days. The fundamentals are the same: pressure changes, edge and turning movements. Your first few attempts at the parallel will inevitably be a little shaky, but remember that you are already familiar with these techniques.

LEFT: *The skis remain parallel throughout the turn. Remember the basic posture positions and make sure that you adopt them when you attempt the move. Note that as you go round the turn you are finely balancing downhill force against the pressure exerted on the skis. As in the other turns you have learnt, this flexes the ski and steers you across the slope, keeping the skis parallel all the way into and out of the fall line.*

The parallel turn

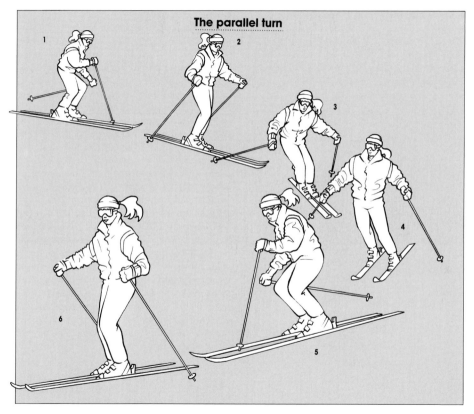

LEFT: *Good preparation and looking well ahead will assist you in the parallel turn. This diagram shows the turn being achieved with the help of the ski poles. Some beginners may prefer not to try to use these tools yet, and indeed it does not matter if the poles are ignored for the first few tries. Prepare to turn 1 by sinking at the knees and ankles. Then 2 extend the legs upwards. The next stage is to turn the legs in the desired direction and at the same time change edges 3. Now turn the skis out of the fall line and into the new direction 4. At this point angulation plays a key role. Having successfully accomplished the turn, you can afford to look ahead and plan your next turn 5 and 6.*

DAY/7

RIGHT: *Remember to keep the skis at hip width apart during these first parallel turns, as this will help your balance. Note the amount of edge being applied here, also the inward tilt of the legs, and at how the body is facing the direction of travel. You can also see the ski poles in use. So far you have not needed to use ski poles in your turns, but in the parallel they help enormously as a timing, balance and coordination tool (see page 58). Using poles may feel strange at first, but when you become familiar with how, when and where to plant and use them, they become like part of your body.*

ROUTES TO THE PARALLEL

There are many ways of achieving the parallel turn. One is to continue with the basic swing, gradually narrowing the plough glide in the fall line. Some alternative methods follow, and all are worth investigating.

Plough to parallel

To use the plough to parallel method you must be reasonably agile as it calls for considerable strength in the legs. However, you still do not need to have the strength of a weightlifter! Anyone of average fitness and strength can do it. It relies on good flexion, rhythm, swift pressure, edge transfer and steering qualities.

Start in a narrow gliding plough facing down the fall line. The turns will not be linked by a traverse, but will snake in and out of the fall line. Look down the slope, and visualize a narrow corridor which sets the boundaries for your turns. Your first turn from this plough glide should be very positive. Continue down the fall line making turn after turn and build up a rhythm of continual plough turns. As you build up speed, more pressure and edge must be applied to the skis to harness the power of momentum. It will help in this if you make a rising and sinking movement, sinking when pressure is needed and rising when the skis need to be light for turning. Maintain the rhythm, flexion and extension and eventually the skis will start to come parallel. As they do, more effort will be required, so the turns will have to be quite punchy and dynamic to ensure good edge and pressure on the skis – which is why reasonable strength is also needed to work the skis in this method.

Plough to parallel

START IN A
NARROW PLOUGH

SINK

SINK

RISE

LEFT: *Find a long and well-pisted slope that is not too steep. Begin in a plough glide position, and start by making a series of short, punchy turns. You may find it easier to rise and sink with the knees and ankles to provide more pressure and reduce weight on the skis. Remember the basic turning ingredients: pressure, edge and turning. As you build up a rhythm, you will feel the inside ski trying to turn parallel to the lower one; let this happen and the skis become parallel. Keeping up the flow and controlling the resistance is the key to the direct method, and this requires practice.*

DAY/7

RIGHT: *When you extend during the traverse, hopping the skis, do so from the legs so that they are projecting you upwards. Do not try to extend from the waist by throwing your body upwards. Try a few hops on the flat at first. Imagine that you have to let the legs hang in the air when you hop. Do not try to pull the legs up into your body as this upsets the balance and finishes in a heavy, hard landing.*

FAR RIGHT: *Flex the legs slightly on landing to absorb the impact. The legs should act like a spring, compressing on landing and extending when you hop.*

Hopping – the basic parallel

It really helps if you are naturally athletic for this method, which involves a hop to free the ski from the snow, and turning the legs in mid-air to change direction. This is obviously a dynamic and energetic turn.

First, try a series of hops as you traverse, keeping the skis going across the slope. When you feel comfortable at this, try one turn. Start from a traverse and in a low position hop at the desired point. While the skis are in the air, turn them in the required direction. In this turn you will need to be aware of the direction of travel and be prepared to compensate for its momentum when you turn the skis. As you turn them, allow your body to angulate and keep balanced over your skis. Try the method the first few times on a very shallow, gentle slope. As you become more proficient, gradually reduce the hop to merely an extension of the legs, keeping the skis in contact with the snow. Do not try to extend from the waist, however.

Removing the inner ski

This is the method for gentle folk! It should be effortless, as long as you have completed the exercises of your first three days and understand angulation. The removal of the inside ski is very much a 'mind over matter' turn, like the passive turn. It will not produce a parallel turn instantly, but it will help get you there. The method is also useful for skiers who wish to eliminate any small wedge occurring during their turns.

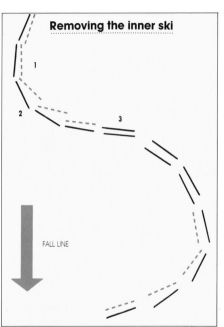

Removing the inner ski

1

2   3

FALL LINE

ABOVE: *From a steep traverse, start by pressurizing the top ski, then gradually turn the inner ski **1** in the direction you wish to go.*

*Angulate here **2** and ensure there is no weight on the top ski (see the photograph on the left). The skis are parallel at the end of the turn **3**.*

The parallel

○ *Change your ski edges simultaneously in the parallel. If the edge change occurs separately, you will not have achieved a true parallel turn.*

○ *Extend the legs for a basic parallel from the knees and ankles, not the waist.*

○ *In the direct method, get a rhythm going and ensure a long run for continuity.*

○ *Practise sensing the momentum and balance against it when turning.*

○ *Look ahead, not down at your skis.*

○ *When turning the inside leg, be sure to lighten it by angulating over the lower ski.*

57

RIGHT: *Before you begin to use the poles, try some simple exercises in the traverse position. As you traverse across the slope, try planting the downhill pole into the snow. As you do this, flex at the knees and ankles. The pole should make contact with the snow when you are at your lowest point. Avoid reaching down with the arms when planting the pole as this will upset your balance and you will not do what you are aiming to do. Once you are more familiar with using the poles, try to bring them into play as you prepare to start your turns, building up a rhythm combining use of poles with turns.*

POLE PLANT

At first you may have found your ski poles something of a hindrance, always getting in the way. By now you should feel quite comfortable with them, and it is worth working on your technique with them, for they are valuable tools. Poles help with balance, timing and rhythm when turning, and they give support at other times.

It is important that you have the correct length of pole and you can test this in the following way. Stand on a flat snow surface, holding a pole by the handle, and push it into the snow from the tip to the basket (it should not go any further). Look at your forearm to see if it is parallel with the ground. If the poles are too long, you may find that they throw you back even when you are using them correctly. If they are too short you will be forced to stoop too low during turns, flexing at the waist rather than at the knees and ankles.

Early on in your skiing career, you should take a very simple approach to using your poles. You use the left one when you want to turn left, and the right one for turning right. Remember that poles are used for balance and to give support. Avoid pointing the pole tips in front of you as it is possible that they could catch in the snow and throw you back.

READING THE TERRAIN

Pick your route as you go and try to read the terrain well ahead. It is all too easy to look down at your skis, but this will only lead to anxiety and tension. As with driving a car, if you look well ahead, you can anticipate difficulties and you have time to take action to deal with them. An example of when you need to plan ahead is when you are on a slope covered in bumps (moguls). Do not try to read the bumps too far ahead when you are beginning, just read two or three at a time. Ice on the piste can also be a hazard but, again, if you have time, you can prepare for it.

RIGHT: *Note how the skier is looking well ahead and keeping his head up – not peering down at his skis. Try to read the terrain that you are heading for, and not just the few yards in front of you. Your line of travel is downwards and across – not simply straight in the direction that your skis are pointed. Monitor slightly to the sides, too.*

Snow conditions

It is not possible to list here all the different types of snow conditions that you are likely to find on the mountain. As you build your experience you will learn to identify and deal with different kinds of conditions, but be particularly careful in your first few days.

The condition that skiers dislike most is ice. This can provide very little grip, and therefore you should ensure that your ski edges are reasonably sharp. Keep calm and try not to tense up. It is best to side slip to an area where the snow gives you more of a grip.

The best condition for learning to ski is firm snow on the piste, for here the skis have plenty to grip on. A well-groomed piste offers the smoothest skiing.

The gem of all conditions is powder snow. If you are lucky enough to find yourself in a resort where there has been a recent fall of snow, get out in it! However, you should note that powder snow is generally skied off the piste and can therefore be treacherous. Here, above all, do not ski away from the piste markers.

If it rains, the snow will change from soft and wet to slushy in a few minutes. Such a surface is potentially very dangerous as the snow becomes very heavy, forming a dense mass rather like wet concrete, so you should avoid it as much as you can.

Reading the terrain

○ *Plan your route, avoiding areas that are marked as difficult. Do not ski away from the piste markers.*
○ *Read the terrain well and anticipate any problems or route changes.*
○ *Look ahead, not down at your skis.*
○ *Remember to monitor slightly to the sides as well as straight ahead.*
○ *If you are confronted with ice, keep calm and try not to tense up. Try to slip to a less icy area.*
○ *Avoid skiing in bad snow conditions; check at the lift station before you go.*

THE FOLLOW UP

RIGHT: *The dry ski slope is a good place to keep your skiing muscles working and for practising your skills. Dry ski slopes offer many different types of ski courses to suit all abilities, from beginners to advanced skiers and even instructors. Ski racing is a popular event on most slopes, attracting keen and competitive racers. Of course you do not have to attend a course or be a racer to get on to the dry ski slope, but for your own and others' safety, you will be asked to prove your skiing ability before you use the facility unsupervised. You have the skills, now get out and have some fun!*

What comes next? Keeping fit some might say. The main thing is to remember the feeling of sliding on snow; it is the same as learning to ride a bicycle – you never forget! There are some other ways to keep ski technique in the fore-front of your mind. Dry ski slopes, which offer the chance to ski all year round, are popular in the UK and are gaining in popularity elsewhere in the world. Some countries have ski fitness machines to help generate that 'ski feeling', and skiing in the summer is possible – and enticing – at higher resorts with a glacier.

Ski resorts

Plan your next ski trip very carefully. The best place for collecting resort information is a travel agent, and the winter season brochures are distributed from the preceding summer. Look out for a good snow record at the resort. A high ski area is preferable, as some low areas suffer from a lack of good snow late in the season. However, these lower areas may have superb skiing through the trees, which higher resorts do not offer. Some resorts provide transport to higher areas. Older ski villages are strong on traditional entertainment, while new resorts may offer skiing right from the door.

After your first week, look for a resort catering for all grades, but which specializes in skiing for intermediate skiers.

The standard of tuition can make or break your trip. Check that you will understand the language, and that instructors are qualified.

LEFT: *Now that you have been bitten by the skiing bug, the planning of the next trip takes precedence over all other priorities! You will enjoy it all the more if you keep yourself reasonably fit for the new season. Remember to pay a few visits to a dry ski slope if you have one near you to remind yourself of what skiing feels like and to hone your technique. It might be worth having some lessons to improve your abilities before the next skiing holiday.*

Whatever your age and ability, skiing is for all. You will be able to ski into your older years provided that you take it at your own pace and enjoy it. The skiing bug is a persistent breed, once it has you, it is unlikely to want to let you go!

GLOSSARY

There are many terms and phrases used in skiing; this glossary will help to explain some of them. But don't let technical fine points confuse you. Keep things simple and enjoy this exciting sport.

Active turning Dynamic pressurizing of the lower ski to initiate turn.

Angulation An outward leaning of the upper body and an inward tilt of the legs to compensate for momentum.

Banking Leaning the whole body in towards the slope during turns.

Basic swing Turning skis to parallel while turning across the slope.

Beginners' slope A ski area with a gentle gradient for learning, masked in green on European ski maps.

Bindings Mechanical device that holds you onto your skis.

Boots A soft inner shell with a stiff outer covering. Front-entry types allow good fit as each clip can be adjusted individually. Rear-entry types are easier to put on and take off and are more common in hire shops.

Button lift Mechanical ski lift for uphill transport which works by towing the skier along on the snow surface.

Chair lift 'High level' cable on which are suspended 'chairs' for up hill transport.

Din table International standard table giving the correct retention settings for ski bindings based on a skier's weight, age and skiing ability.

Downhill The 'lower' ski or term for the area below the skier.

Dry slope Plastic bristle surface used as a ski area for practice. Common in the UK and growing in popularity elsewhere.

Edges Metal strips along both sides of the ski base enabling turning and grip.

Fall line Most direct line of least resistance down the hill.

Flexing Bending at the joints or making the ski bend.

Flow Free movement with resistance.

Gliding Control of speed through 'flow and resist'.

Goggles Bad weather eye protection.

Heel piece Ski binding securing the heel section of the ski boot. The brake is incorporated here.

Herringbone Method of walking straight up hill with skis on.

Hopping Extension of legs from a flexed position resulting in the skis leaving the ground.

Leg turning Turning of leg from the hip joint while moving on skis.

Maps In European resorts, difficulty of ski runs is indicated by colour (green, blue, red and black) on a ski map; in the US, names are used.

Moguls Bumps on the slope's surface made of compacted snow 'spraying' from other skiers.

Momentum Impetus gained from motion on skis.

Nursery slope Ski area for beginners (see *Beginners' slope*).

Parallel Skis at equal distance along their length.

Passive turning Removing weight/pressure from top ski to initiate turn.

Piste Ski run area with a prepared surface defined by coloured markers. Track or boundary for route of descent.

Planting Moment at which ski pole makes contact with the snow when used in ski turns.

Plough brake Increase in resistance in a plough position resulting in a halt.

Plough glide Skis in a 'V' shape sliding freely down the hill.

Poles Ski poles used for balance, timing and support.

Powder snow Light, very dry, fresh snow.

Resist Opposing the flow created by momentum.

Run out Area at foot of slope, either a counter slope or flat section.

Salopettes Ski trousers. Good ski wear includes a waterproof membrane, which allows the body to breathe.

Shuss Sliding with the skis parallel directly down the fall line.

Side step Method of walking sideways up the slope with skis on.

Side slipping Slipping sideways down the fall line (direct); slipping sideways diagonally across the fall line (diagonal).

Side skidding Momentum induced skid sideways.

Sinking Lowering of body by bending at the knees and ankles to assist pressurizing of the turning ski.

Ski brake Device incorporated into the bindings, designed to stop the ski should it become detached from the skier.

Ski base Underside of ski sole area, usually plastic, in contact with the snow surface.

Slopes Ski area on the side of a mountain.

Snowplough Legs and feet are used to move the tails of the skis apart and rotate the skis

slightly inwards, thus 'ploughing' the snow out of the way. The wider the 'V' position, the slower the skier will travel.

Stance The position of the body. A relaxed posture and well-balanced position is vital. The body should be in an 'S' shape to allow flexibility.

Straight running Moving with the skis parallel, facing directly down the fall line (see *Shuss*).

'T'–bar lift Mode of uphill transport which tows two people at a time along the snow's surface.

Tails Rear portion of the skis.

Terrain The mountain slope, with its varied snow conditions, ridges, bumps and hollows.

Tips Curved, pointed, front of skis.

Toe piece Front section of ski binding which holds the toe of the ski boot.

Traverse Moving diagonally across the slope.

Turns Change of direction from existing line.

Wedge position Skis close at the tips and wide at the tails (similar to snowplough).

INDEX

● ●

Notes: Primary treatment of subjects is indicated by **bold** page numbers; information contained in captions and annotations by *italic*; textual references are in normal type.

Index by Stuart Craik